NATURE KNOWS !

THE BIRDS' TALENT SHOW

MARINA SHATS

ISBN: 1-4819-8896-4
ISBN-13: 9781481988964

The Birds' Talent Show

Once upon a time there was a Birds' Talent Festival in Italy. This famous festival was organized by a wise, old Crow named Carr. During her long life, she had seen hundreds of different birds. She had heard their songs and saw their fantastic dances. She saw many wonderful birds whose appearance captivated everyone. She was sure that there were more talented and beautiful birds in the world.

When she thought this, Carr decided that the birds of the world should have their own talent festival and began the task of inviting all the birds of the world to such an unusual event.

One spring morning, the birds all over the world found a note in their nests.

It read:

My dear feathered friends: I have what you do not and you have what I do not. If we get together, we would all be able to share. You are invited to a grand festival of the birds at Happy Valley on July 26, at 1:00 p.m. You have one full year to prepare for the Festival. Prepare yourselves for your performance of a lifetime. Try to train hard! Please arrive promptly because there's no reserved seating and we expect the seats to fill quickly. I look forward to seeing you there. Good luck!"

The Penguins were not invited. They couldn't fly and Carr never thought of going all the way to Antarctica to invite them, but everyone in the world loves penguins. Workers of the zoo near Happy Valley learned about the Festival and passed the invitation to the Penguins in their zoo. They trained the Penguins to dance.

A year later, thousands of the birds flew to the Festival. There, they found a large bulletin board with the following announcement:

"Dear guests! Please be ready to perform at the opening. Clean, wash, preen and primp yourself. If you have crowns or beards, or showy tails, don't hide them! Do not be afraid to show your legs. Shine your claws and bills. If you need assistance, experienced hairdressers and manicurists are on duty. We have a variety of food for all of you."

The birds started looking around and introducing themselves.

The next morning, the town criers, who were the roosters, started going through the valley crowing, "Cock-a-doodle-do! It is time for the Festival! Come and join us for a delightful breakfast!" During the feast, the birds heard an announcement over the intercom: "Ladies and gentlemen, attention, please! We are starting our Festival after our breakfast. You will be able watch and listen to a concert of the most famous performers. There are trees, bushes and grasses there. There, you can choose your seats. Admission is free."

At the last minute, the disable turkey appeared on the plaza. He came as a visitor, because he heard about the show and would like to see it. The Penguins marched to the plaza from the zoo.

When the birds had found their seats, the impresario, a bald eagle, stepped onto the stage and up to the microphone:

"Dear friends, we would like to start our Festival. You can sit and stand, but please be quiet. We ask that you do not drink, eat or talk. You can smile, but refrain from loud laughter because some of us could be frightened. Now, let me introduce you to one of the best singers in the world."

A Nightingale fluttered onto the stage singing several songs in warble. His first song was in a high-pitched warble. The guests loved his voice and gave him a great round of applause. He sang as an encore a few of his favorite songs, which the audience also loved. Gracefully, he rose up and flew away.

Next to perform was a group of Penguins. They danced a waltz. The Woodpeckers, Spoonbills, and Cuckoos stepped to the stage next. The Woodpeckers drummed, the Spoonbills snapped their bills in pizzicato imitating them, and the Cuckoos accompanied with their "Coo-coo." The captivating choir of Crows cawed, joining the ensemble.

The audience flapped their wings loudly following each performance. Then, the Cranes danced a jazz dance.

Between each performance, the audience flapped their wings in loud appreciation. This drowned out the snoring of the owls. Otherwise, the owls could be heard almost all the time.

Awards were granted to the winners in each category. The first prize for singers was given to the Nightingale. The first prize for dancers was given to Cranes.

First place awards included a best pre-made nest, tickets to the Arctic, and feather make-up.

At the last moment of the festival, a large flock of Sparrows flew up to the stage. All of them had notes in their bills. They scattered the notes between the guests.

The notes read:

"Dear friends, you seemed enjoy the Festival, but you did not know who the organizer of it was. It was the Crow, named Carr, who prepared and delivered the invitations all over the world. She is the grand prize winner of the Festival!"

"We want Carr, we want Carr" demanded the birds. So Carr came to the stage. She was very shy and couldn't say a word, but the sparrows slowly flew around her and chirped with their gentle voices.

The grant prize, a bag full of the best seed in the world, was presented to Carr. "Congratulations, dear Carr! We would like to do this again and again!" chirped the Sparrows.

All the guests rose and applauded Carr. She bowed several times, cawed with excitement, and quickly hopped off the stage.

At the end of the Festival, the whole audience was invited to dance. Inspired guests took each other's wings, and danced in the air. There was no end to the gaiety. The dancing lasted until 4:00 in the morning.

The Festival was finally over. All the guests flew back to their Homelands, and the Penguins returned to the zoo.

The End

Dandelion

Once upon a time, there was a magical kingdom called Flower Land. It was called Flower Land because its fields and meadows were covered with beautiful flowers. Like everywhere else in the world, spring came every year to this land. The sun woke up Flower Land from its winter's nap with warm, shiny golden rays. Nature started to wake up and come alive. The meadows and fields began to bloom. Brooks babbled and birds returned from faraway places. Bees and dragonflies buzzed about; butterflies flew; crickets chirped, and new flowers appeared.

One spring, a little flower appeared in one of the meadows. He had a fluffy, yellow head on the top of a thin stem. He was very glad to be alive and was glad to be in this magical land. Even though his head flopped a lot, he thought that this was normal and he really was just like the other flowers.

He liked to gather his friends near him by telling jokes and funny stories.

Everybody liked to be near and listen to him; even though he was not as attractive as the other flowers in this country. They did not care about his looks.

A wise old bee, named Mora, took a liking to him. She told him many stories about their wonderful land.

She told him a story about the beautiful princess who was actually a pink flower with transparent petals who smelled wonderful.

"Once upon a time," began Mora, "a lovely Princess Rose, lived in our land. When the birds flew to other places during the wintertime, they spread the news about the beauty of their Princess."

Mora continued: "Once, an old witch who was shaped like a big gray cloud and lived in damp kingdom not far away, heard about the beautiful Princess. The witch had two daughters, who also appeared as light gray clouds. The witch wanted to see just how beautiful this Princess really was. So she traveled to where the Princess lived, looked her over carefully and then saw that the Princess was really beautiful. She resented the fact that everybody liked the Princess, but did not like her ugly daughters."

"I will give my daughters a gift," the witch said. "I will take the Princess to my kingdom. When my daughters look at her, they will think she is a mirror and they will think they are as beautiful as the Princess."

Mora told the flower: "The witch put a spell on the Princess and she promptly fell into a deep sleep. While she slept, the witch took her to the damp kingdom. Then she asked her daughters to guard the beautiful flower Princess."

Her daughters were excited to have this gift. They saw themselves as beautiful as the Princess Rose.

"Mother, thank you for such a present," they said to the witch.

"It is my pleasure! I hope my daughters will soon be as famous as a Princess and that everybody in the world will want to see you again and again! This was and is my goal," she replied.

"Meanwhile, all the flowers in the Flower Land worried about their missing Princess," the bee added sadly. "But I knew the Princess could be saved. All she needed was the most handsome flower-prince from our land to rescue her," she finished.

The yellow flower was so taken with Mora's story that he told Mora that he wanted to rescue the Princess. Mora didn't say anything and flew away.

One day after a rain, the babbling brook grew and came closer to the yellow flower. Unexpectedly, the flower saw his reflection and realized that he was not as attractive as other flowers in the Flower Land.

"What could I do to save the Princess?" he thought to himself. When he saw the bee again, he told her: "I am not as handsome as most handsome princes should be in our country, and I am not even a prince."

Knowing about his looks upset him even more. He was sure that his dream to save the princess would never come true and he felt very sad. His friends did not recognize him anymore. No one heard him tell jokes or stories. He did not smile or enjoy seeing nature around him. Slowly, his yellow head began to turn white and he started looking like a Dandelion. However, he had one more Friend and that was the sun. Each morning the Sun tried to help him by warming him with her gold rays.

"Please help me," the Dandelion asked the sun. The sun responded: "I would like to help you. What do you want most of all?

I need to save the beautiful princess and I would like to be the most handsome prince of all.

The Summer began again in the magic land, but the Dandelion was still unhappy; he couldn't forger about the sleeping princess. He only thought about her.

The rays of the kind sun worked magic. One morning, the Dandelion's friends didn't recognize him at all. The saw a handsome flower on a high, graceful stem. On his floppy white locks flashed a tiny crown.

"Oh, this must be our prince! We have never had such handsome prince in our land! "Congratulations, our Prince!"

The Prince Dandelion smiled at last. He understood that he had become the most handsome prince of all Princes.

However, his dream to save the Princess wouldn't fade away. Day and night he thought "How can I go to that gloomy kingdom?"

One morning, just when the sun had started to rise slowly over the world, two light gray clouds floated above the sun rays and glided over the land. Suddenly, the Prince imagined that the beautiful Princess was sleeping in the sky near those two clouds.

"Don't leave!" was all he had time to say before everything in the sky disappeared in the morning mist.

The Prince Dandelion began to feel sad again.

"I would like to die. Then, my soul would rise to the sky. Only then would it be possible for me to see the beauty," he told his friends.

The Prince Dandelion continued to feel unhappy; his fluffy head dropped and began to be thinner. Little by little, all of his fluffy hair fell off and scattered all over the world. The wind took one little bit of his hair and brought it to the sky.

The next morning, his friends didn't find him. They saw only the stem. On the ground, near the stem, the crown, flashed brightly. It was all that left of the Prince. Everybody was disappointed. No one was able to see the Prince Dandelion again.

The seed of the fluff which the wind took to the sky was the soul of the Prince. Just by chance, it ended in the gloomy, damp kingdom where the beautiful Princess Rose slept.

Spring came again, and the kind sun worked as hard as ever. Once, when she got tired, she decided to rest and lied down for a while near two light grey clouds that were floating nearby. They were the grey daughters of the witch from the gloomy, damp kingdom where the beautiful Princess Rose was still sleeping and the Prince Dandelion had landed the year before, and slept until the return of the spring.

Just then, when the sun's rays touched the clouds, a yellow flower began to grow from the white bit of his soul.

"Oh, this is the Prince Dandelion from the Flower Land!" she said, because she recognized him immediately. The sun became very happy, and her rays began to shine more and more. Under her magical, warm rays Prince Dandelion grew.

One morning, the yellow head became delightfully white and fluffy. Yes, it was Prince Dandelion who had come to life. He was very happy to look at nature around him. Just then, quite unexpectedly, he noticed a very pretty pink flower with transparent petals that was sleeping near him. She smelled wonderful. On her gentle head flashed a small gold crown. The Prince understood that he had gotten his wish at last.

It was really Princess Rose from their magical land! The Prince slowly bent over her and gently kissed her face. The pink flower opened her beautiful eyes and smiled.

Yes, his dream came true at last!

"Thank you, dear Prince! I saw you many times in my dreams, but I didn't know that you would really come. Again, thank you!" Princess Rose said.

The light gray clouds who were the daughters of the witch that were guarding the Princess got very upset because they were afraid of their mother. They changed from light gray and then to rain.

The Prince Dandelion held the beauty close to him, and they came down to earth of the steam of rain (the boat of love).

This was their fairy tale land! There was a wedding with lots of guests and presents. Bee Mora also flew to the wedding. The very best presents were from the sun and moon. The sun gave some of her rays, which were used to make the wedding dress for Princess Rose. The moon also gave some of her rays, which were used to make the wedding suit of Prince Dandelion.

The prince and princess lived happily ever and had many beautiful children with beautiful pink and white heads.

The end

Flower People

Once upon a time there was a Flower country somewhere on the Earth. This country was far away from other countries and no one knew about it. I should say no one big knew about it, for it was filled with tiny little people. These people were smaller than any of the flowers. This was the only country of this kind in the world.

The people liked the Flower country, their homeland. They used flowers for many different occasions. They found ways to use each season's flowers. For example, during the summer, the little people used the small pond for swimming.

There were a lot of lilies, and people used their petals as diving boards to dive from them to the water.

Sometimes, they used lilies for gondolas. They loved to use flowers and play with these beautiful flowers that way.

During the sunny warm days they liked to lie and rest on the heads of Dandelions, which had gone to seed, because they are soft and convenient to be used as a resting place.

Some of the little people used the Sunflowers to sit on because of their name. In fact, they would take their umbrellas with them. If it wasn't that sunny, they didn't care because they were sitting on the Sunflower with an umbrella.

During the rain, the little people found the flowers acted like umbrellas.

During the winter, the flower people practiced ice- skating on lilies.

Also, during the winter months, the little people rested at their shelters and went to practice their music and dances. They used the Ornamental Cabbages as their floor to keep from getting muddy.

Some girls used a flower as a hat.

Every year the little people grew older and became young adults. The teenage boys began to make dates with teenage girls.

The boys asked their loved ones to marry them. In this country there was a tradition to invite guests by blowing a musical invitation through a trumpeter flower.

The Tulips were used as a platform as a stand for the groom and bride. The guests would stand under the Tulips and congratulate the bride and groom on their marriage.

The end